COOKIES AT HOME

50 Easy-to-Make Ideas for Planning

Healthy and Flavorful Low Fat Meals

Dorothy Allen

Table of Contents

Almond Bars

Amount Measure Ingredient

- ❖ 1 package white cake mix
- ❖ 1/2 cup butter or margarine -- softened
- ❖ 2 eggs
- ❖ Almond Topping -- (recipe follows)

ALMOND TOPPING

- ❖ 2/3 cup sliced almonds
- ❖ 2/3 cup butter or margarine
- ❖ 1/2 cup sugar
- ❖ 1 tablespoon plus 1 teaspoon all-purpose flour
- ❖ 1 tablespoon milk

Preparation Method

Heat oven to 350°. Beat cake mix (dry), butter and eggs with electric mixer on low speed until dough forms or mix with the spoon.

Press in bottom of ungreased jelly roll pan, 15 1/2 × 10 1/2 × 1 inch.

Bake 20 to 25 minutes or until golden brown and crust begins to pull away from sides of pan or until toothpick inserted in centre comes out clean.

Immediately spread Topping over crust. Set oven control to broil. Place pan on middle rack in oven.

Broil 2 to 3 minutes or until Topping is golden brown and bubbly (watch carefully Topping burns easily). Cool completely. Cut into 8 rows by 4 rows.

ALMOND TOPPING:

Cook all ingredients in 2-quart saucepan over low heat, stirring constantly, until sugar is dissolved, and mixture thickens slightly.

Almond Bonbons

- ❖ 1 1/2 cups all-purpose flour

- ❖ 1/2 cup butter or margarine -- softened

- ❖ 1/3 cup powdered sugar

- ❖ 2 tablespoons milk

- ❖ 1/2 teaspoon vanilla

- ❖ 1/2 (7 ounce) package almond paste (7- or 8-ounce size)

- ❖ Almond Glaze -- (recipe follows)

- ❖ Sliced almonds -- toasted, if desired (see Notes)

ALMOND GLAZE

- ❖ 1 cup powdered sugar

- ❖ 1/2 teaspoon almond extract

- ❖ 4 teaspoons milk (4 to 5 teaspoons)

Preparation Method

Heat oven to 375°. Beat flour, butter, powdered sugar, milk and vanilla in large bowl with electric mixer on medium speed or mix with spoon. Cut almond paste into 1/2-inch slices; cut each slice into fourths.

Shape 1-inch ball of dough around each piece of almond paste. Gently roll to form ball. Place about 1 inch apart on ungreased cookie sheet.

Bake 10 to 12 minutes or until set and bottom is golden brown.

Remove from cookie sheet to wire rack. Cool completely.

Dip tops of cookies into the Almond Glaze. Garnish with sliced almonds.

ALMOND GLAZE:

Mix all ingredients until smooth and spreadable.

Almond Macaroons

Amount Measure Ingredient

- ❖ 1 (7 ounce) package almond paste (7 or 8 ounces)
- ❖ 1/4 cup all-purpose flour
- ❖ 1 1/4 cups powdered sugar
- ❖ 1/4 teaspoon almond extract
- ❖ 2 egg whites
- ❖ 3 dozen blanched whole almonds

Preparation Method

Grease cookie sheet. Break almond paste into small pieces in a large bowl. Stir in flour, powdered sugar and the almond extract. Add egg whites. Beat with electric mixer on medium speed about 2 minutes, scraping bowl occasionally, until smooth.

Place dough in decorating bag fitted with #9 rosette tip. Pipe 1 1/2- inch cookies about 2 inches apart onto cookie sheet. Top each with almond. Refrigerate 30 minutes.

Heat oven to 325°. Bake about 12 minutes or until edges are light brown. Immediately remove from cookie sheet to wire rack.

Cool completely. Store in airtight container.

Almond-Filled Crescents

Serving Size: 48   Preparation Time: 0:00

Amount Measure Ingredient

- ❖ 1 cup powdered sugar

- ❖ 1 cup whipping (heavy) cream

- ❖ 2 eggs

- ❖ 3 3/4 cups all-purpose flour

- ❖ 1 teaspoon baking powder

- ❖ 1/2 teaspoon salt

- ❖ 1 (7 ounce) package almond paste (7 or 8 ounces)

- ❖ 3/4 cup butter or margarine -- softened

- ❖ Easy Glaze -- (recipe follows)

EASY GLAZE

- ❖ 1 cup powdered sugar

- ❖ 6 teaspoons milk (6 to 7 teaspoons)

Preparation Method

Mix powdered sugar, whipping cream and the eggs in large bowl with spoon. Stir in flour, baking powder and salt (dough will be stiff). Cover and refrigerate about 1 hour or until firm.

Heat oven to 375°. Break the almond paste into small pieces in medium bowl; add butter. Beat with electric mixer on low speed until blended. Beat on high speed until fluffy (tiny bits of almond paste will remain).

Roll one fourth of dough at a time into 10-inch circle on lightly floured surface. Spread one fourth of almond paste mixture (1/2 cup) over circle. Cut into 12 wedges.

Roll up wedges, beginning at rounded edge. Place on ungreased cookie sheet with points underneath. Repeat with the remaining dough and almond paste mixture. Bake 14 to 16 minutes or until golden brown. Remove from cookie sheet to wire rack.

Cool completely. Drizzle with Glaze.

EASY GLAZE:

Mix ingredients until smooth and thin enough to drizzle.

Animal Cookies

Amount Measure Ingredient

- ❖ 1/2 cup granulated sugar
- ❖ 1/2 cup packed brown sugar
- ❖ 1/2 cup butter or margarine -- softened
- ❖ 1 teaspoon vanilla
- ❖ 1 egg
- ❖ 2 cups all-purpose flour
- ❖ 1 teaspoon baking powder
- ❖ 1/2 teaspoon salt
- ❖ 1/2 teaspoon ground cinnamon

Preparation Method

Heat oven to 350°. Beat sugars, butter, vanilla and egg in large bowl with electric mixer on medium speed or mix with spoon.

Stir in remaining ingredients. (If dough is too soft to shape, cover and refrigerate about 2 hours or until firm.)

Shape dough by 2 tablespoonfuls into slightly flattened balls and ropes. Arrange on ungreased cookie sheet to form animals as desired. Use small pieces of dough for facial features if desired. Bake about 10 to 12 minutes or until edges are golden brown. Remove from cookie sheet to wire rack.

Anise Biscotti

Amount Measure Ingredient

- ❖ 1 cup sugar

- ❖ 1/2 cup butter or margarine -- softened

- ❖ 2 teaspoons anise seed -- ground

- ❖ 2 teaspoons grated lemon peel

- ❖ 2 eggs

- ❖ 3 1/2 cups all-purpose flour

- ❖ 1 teaspoon baking powder

- ❖ 1/2 teaspoon salt

Preparation Method

Heat oven to 350°. Beat sugar, butter, anise seed, lemon peel and eggs in large bowl with electric mixer on medium speed or mix with spoon. Stir in remaining ingredients. Divide dough in half.

Shape each half into rectangle, 10 × 3 inches, on ungreased cookie sheet.

Bake about 20 minutes or until toothpick inserted in centre comes out clean. Cool on cookie sheet 15 minutes.

Cut crosswise into 1/2-inch slices. Turn slices cut sides down on cookie sheet. Bake about 15 minutes or until crisp and light brown. Remove from cookie sheet to wire rack.

Applesauce-Granola Cookies

Amount Measure Ingredient

- ❖ 1 cup packed brown sugar
- ❖ 1/2 cup shortening
- ❖ 1 teaspoon vanilla
- ❖ 1 egg
- ❖ 1/2 cup applesauce
- ❖ 2 cups all-purpose flour
- ❖ 2 cups granola
- ❖ 1/2 teaspoon baking soda
- ❖ 1/2 teaspoon salt

Preparation Method

Heat oven to 375°. Beat brown sugar, shortening, vanilla and egg in large bowl with electric mixer on medium speed, or mix with spoon. Stir in applesauce. Stir in remaining ingredients.

Drop dough by rounded tablespoonfuls about 2 inches apart onto ungreased cookie sheet.

Bake 11 to 13 minutes or until almost no indentation remains when touched in centre. Cool 1 to 2 minutes; remove from cookie sheet to wire rack.

Apricot-Cherry Bars

Amount Measure Ingredient

- ❖ 1 package yellow cake mix
- ❖ 1/4 cup water
- ❖ 1/4 cup butter or margarine -- softened
- ❖ 1/4 cup packed brown sugar
- ❖ 2 eggs
- ❖ 1 cup cut-up dried apricots
- ❖ 1/2 cup drained chopped maraschino cherries
- ❖ Powdered sugar

Preparation Method

Heat oven to 375°. Grease and flour jelly roll pan, 15 1/2 × 10 1/2 × 1 inch. Beat half of the cake mix (dry), the water, butter, brown sugar and eggs in large bowl with electric mixer on medium speed until smooth or mix with spoon.

Stir in remaining cake mix, the apricots and cherries. Spread evenly in pan.

Bake 20 to 25 minutes or until toothpick inserted in centre comes out clean. Cool completely.

Sprinkle with powdered sugar. Cut into 6 rows by 5 rows.

Banana-Cornmeal Cookies

Amount Measure Ingredient

- ❖ 1 cup packed brown sugar

- ❖ 1/2 cup granulated sugar

- ❖ 1/2 cup butter or margarine -- softened

- ❖ 1/2 cup mashed very ripe banana (1 medium)

- ❖ 1 egg

- ❖ 2 1/2 cups all-purpose flour

- ❖ 1 cup yellow cornmeal

- ❖ 1 teaspoon baking powder

- ❖ 1/2 teaspoon salt

- ❖ 1 teaspoon ground cinnamon

- ❖ 1/4 cup granulated sugar

- ❖ 1/2 teaspoon ground cinnamon

Preparation Method

Heat oven to 375°. Grease cookie sheet.

Beat brown sugar, 1/2 cup granulated sugar, butter, banana and egg in large bowl with an electric mixer on medium speed or mix with spoon.

Stir in flour, cornmeal, baking powder, salt and 1 teaspoon cinnamon. (If dough is too soft to shape, cover and refrigerate about 2 hours or until firm.)

Mix 1/4 cup granulated sugar and 1/2 teaspoon cinnamon.

Shape dough into 1 1/4-inch balls. Place about 3 inches apart on cookie sheet. Flatten slightly in crisscross pattern with fork dipped into cinnamon-sugar mixture.

Bake 10 to 12 minutes or until light brown.

Immediately remove from cookie sheet to wire rack.

Banana-Ginger Jumbles

Amount Measure Ingredient

- ❖ 1 cup packed brown sugar
- ❖ 1/2 cup butter or margarine -- softened
- ❖ 1/2 cup shortening
- ❖ 1 tablespoon grated gingerroot OR 1 teaspoon ground ginger*
- ❖ 2 eggs
- ❖ 1 cup mashed very ripe bananas (2 medium)
- ❖ 1/4 cup milk
- ❖ 3 cups all-purpose flour
- ❖ 1 teaspoon baking powder
- ❖ 3/4 teaspoon salt
- ❖ Powdered sugar, if desired

Preparation Method

Heat oven to 375°.

Beat brown sugar, butter, shortening, gingerroot, and eggs in large bowl with electric mixer on medium speed or mix with spoon. Stir in bananas and milk. Stir in flour, baking powder and salt.

Drop dough by rounded tablespoonfuls about 2 inches apart onto ungreased cookie sheet.

Bake 9 to 11 minutes or until almost no indentation remains when touched in centre.

Remove from cookie sheet to wire rack. Sprinkle with powdered sugar while warm.

Banana-Nut Bars

Amount Measure Ingredient

- ❖ 1 cup sugar
- ❖ 1 cup mashed very ripe bananas (2 medium)
- ❖ 1/3 cup vegetable oil
- ❖ 2 eggs
- ❖ 1 cup all-purpose flour
- ❖ 1 teaspoon baking powder
- ❖ 1/2 teaspoon baking soda
- ❖ 1/2 teaspoon ground cinnamon
- ❖ 1/4 teaspoon salt
- ❖ 1/2 cup chopped nuts
- ❖ Cream Cheese Frosting -- (recipe follows)

CREAM CHEESE FROSTING

- ❖ 1 (3 ounce) package cream cheese -- softened
- ❖ 1/3 cup butter or margarine -- softened
- ❖ 1 teaspoon vanilla

❖ 2 cups powdered sugar

Preparation Method

Heat oven to 350°. Grease rectangular pan, 13 × 9 × 2 inches. Mix sugar, bananas, oil and eggs in large bowl with spoon.

Stir in flour, baking powder, baking soda, cinnamon and salt. Stir in nuts.

Spread batter in pan. Bake 25 to 30 minutes or until toothpick inserted in centre comes out clean. Cool completely.

Frost with Cream Cheese Frosting.

Cut into 6 rows by 4 rows. Store covered in refrigerator.

CREAM CHEESE FROSTING:

Mix cream cheese, butter and vanilla in medium bowl. Gradually beat in powdered sugar with spoon until smooth and spreadable.

Black-Eyed Susans

Amount Measure Ingredient

- ❖ 3/4 cup butter or margarine -- softened
- ❖ 1/2 cup sugar
- ❖ 1 teaspoon vanilla
- ❖ 12 drops yellow food color
- ❖ 1 egg
- ❖ 1 (3 ounce) package cream cheese -- softened
- ❖ 2 cups all-purpose flour
- ❖ 3 dozen (about) large semisweet chocolate chips

Preparation Method

Beat butter, sugar, vanilla, food color, egg and cream cheese in large bowl with electric mixer on medium speed or mix with spoon. Stir in flour. Cover and refrigerate about 2 hours or until firm.

Heat oven to 375°. Shape dough into 1 1/4-inch balls.

Place about 2 inches apart on ungreased cookie sheet.

Make 3 cuts with scissors in top of each ball about three-fourths of the way through to make 6 wedges.

Spread wedges apart slightly to form flower petals (cookies will flatten as they bake).

Bake 10 to 12 minutes or until set and edges begin to brown.

Immediately press 1 chocolate chip in centre of each cookie.

Remove from cookie sheet to wire rack. Cut balls from top into 6 wedges about 3/4 way through dough.

Brandied Fruit Drops

Amount Measure Ingredient

- ❖ 3/4 cup packed brown sugar

- ❖ 1/2 cup butter or margarine -- softened

- ❖ 1/3 cup brandy

- ❖ 2 eggs

- ❖ 2 cups all-purpose flour

- ❖ 2 teaspoons baking powder

- ❖ 1 teaspoon ground cardamom

- ❖ 1/2 teaspoon ground cinnamon

- ❖ 1/2 teaspoon ground nutmeg

- ❖ 1 cup chopped pecans

- ❖ 1 cup dried apricots -- chopped

- ❖ 1/2 cup currants

- ❖ 1/2 cup golden raisins

Preparation Method

Heat oven to 350°. Grease cookie sheet. Beat brown sugar, butter, brandy and the eggs in large bowl with electric mixer on medium speed or mix with spoon.

Stir in flour, baking powder, cardamom, cinnamon and nutmeg. Stir in remaining ingredients.

Drop dough by rounded teaspoonfuls about 2 inches apart onto cookie sheet.

Bake 9 to 11 minutes or until light brown. Remove from cookie sheet to wire rack.

Brandy Snap Cups

Amount Measure Ingredient

- ❖ 1/4 cup butter or margarine
- ❖ 1/4 cup dark corn syrup
- ❖ 2 tablespoons plus 2 teaspoons brown sugar
- ❖ 1 teaspoon brandy
- ❖ 6 tablespoons all-purpose flour
- ❖ 1/4 teaspoon ground ginger
- ❖ 4 cups mixed fresh strawberries and raspberries
- ❖ 2/3 cup raspberry jam -- melted

Preparation Method

Heat oven to 350°. Heat butter, corn syrup and brown sugar to boiling in 1 1/2-quart saucepan, stirring frequently; remove from heat. Stir in brandy.

Mix flour and ginger; gradually stir into syrup mixture.

Drop dough by heaping teaspoonfuls at least 5 inches apart onto lightly greased cookie sheets or line sheets with baking parchment paper.

Bake until cookies have spread into 4- or 5-inch rounds and are golden brown, 3 to 4 minutes (watch carefully as these cookies brown quickly).

Cool cookies 1 to 3 minutes before removing from cookie sheets.

Working quickly, shape over inverted drinking glass about 2 to 2 ½ inches in diameter. Allow cookies to harden; remove gently and place on wire racks. Cool completely.

If cookies become too crisp to shape, return to oven to soften about 1 minute.

Fill each cookie cup with ¼ cup berries. Drizzle with jam.

Brown Sugar Drops

Amount Measure Ingredient

- ❖ 2 cups packed brown sugar
- ❖ 1/2 cup butter or margarine -- softened
- ❖ 1/2 cup shortening
- ❖ 1/2 cup milk
- ❖ 2 eggs
- ❖ 3 1/2 cups all-purpose flour
- ❖ 1 teaspoon baking soda
- ❖ 1/2 teaspoon salt

Light Brown Glaze -- (recipe follows)

LIGHT BROWN GLAZE

- ❖ 4 cups powdered sugar
- ❖ 1/2 cup butter or margarine -- melted
- ❖ 2 teaspoons vanilla
- ❖ 2 tablespoons milk (2 to 4 tablespoons)

Preparation Method

Heat oven to 400°. Beat brown sugar, butter, shortening, milk and eggs in large bowl with electric mixer on medium speed or mix with spoon. Stir in flour, baking soda and salt.

Drop dough by rounded tablespoonfuls about 2 inches apart onto ungreased cookie sheet.

Bake 9 to 11 minutes or until almost no indentation remains when touched in centre. Cool 1 to 2 minutes; remove from cookie sheet to wire rack.

Cool completely. Spread with Light Brown Glaze.

LIGHT BROWN GLAZE:

Mix all ingredients until smooth and spreadable.

Brownie Crinkles

Amount Measure Ingredient

❖ 1 package Sweet Rewards® low-fat

❖ fudge brownie mix

❖ 1/4 cup water

❖ 1/4 cup fat-free, cholesterol-free egg product

OR

❖ 1 egg

❖ 1/2 cup powdered sugar

Preparation Method

Heat oven to 350°. Grease cookie sheet. Mix brownie mix (dry), water and egg product with spoon about 50 strokes or until well blended.

Shape dough by rounded teaspoonfuls into balls. Roll in powdered sugar. Place about 2 inches apart on cookie sheet.

Bake 10 to 12 minutes or until almost no indentation remains when touched lightly in centre.

Immediately remove from cookie sheet to wire rack.

Brownie Drop Cookies

Amount Measure Ingredient

- ❖ 1 (15 ounce) package fudge brownie mix
- ❖ 1/4 cup water
- ❖ 1 egg
- ❖ 1/2 cup chopped nuts

Preparation Method

Heat oven to 375°. Lightly grease cookie sheet. Mix brownie mix, water and egg in large bowl with spoon.

Stir in nuts (dough will be stiff).

Drop dough by rounded teaspoonfuls onto cookie sheet.

Bake 6 to 8 minutes or until set.

Cool slightly; remove from cookie sheet to wire rack.

Bumblebees

Amount Measure Ingredient

- ❖ 1/2 cup peanut butter

- ❖ 1/2 cup shortening

- ❖ 1/3 cup packed brown sugar

- ❖ 1/3 cup honey

- ❖ 1 egg

- ❖ 1 3/4 cups all-purpose flour

- ❖ 3/4 teaspoon baking soda

- ❖ 1/2 teaspoon baking powder

- ❖ 8 dozen pretzel twists

- ❖ 8 dozen pretzel sticks

Preparation Method

Beat peanut butter, shortening, brown sugar, honey and egg in large bowl with electric mixer on medium speed, or mix with spoon.

Stir in flour, baking soda and baking powder. Cover dough with plastic wrap and refrigerate about 2 hours or until firm.

Heat oven to 350°. Shape dough into 1-inch balls (dough will be slightly sticky).

For each cookie, place two pretzel twists side by side with the bottoms (the bottom comes to a rounded point, like the bottom of a heart shape) touching on ungreased cookie sheet.

Place 1 ball of dough on centre and flatten slightly. Break 2 pretzel sticks in half.

Gently press three pretzel stick halves into dough for stripes on bee.

Break fourth pretzel piece in half. Poke pieces into one end of dough for antennae.

Bake 11 to 13 minutes or until light golden brown.

Immediately remove from cookie sheet to wire rack.

Butter Crunch Clusters

Amount Measure Ingredient

- ❖ 1/2 cup butter or margarine

- ❖ 2/3 cup packed brown sugar

- ❖ 1 tablespoon corn syrup

- ❖ 2 cups Cheerios® cereal

- ❖ 1 cup salted cocktail peanuts or Spanish peanuts

Preparation Method

Heat butter in 3-quart saucepan over low heat until melted. Stir in brown sugar and corn syrup.

Heat to boiling over medium heat, stirring constantly. Boil and stir 1 minute; remove from heat.

Stir in cereal and peanuts until well coated. Drop mixture by tablespoonfuls onto waxed paper; cool.

Butterscotch Shortbread

Amount Measure Ingredient

- ❖ 1/2 cup butter or margarine -- softened
- ❖ 1/2 cup shortening
- ❖ 1/2 cup packed brown sugar
- ❖ 1/4 cup granulated sugar
- ❖ 2 1/4 cups all-purpose flour
- ❖ 1 teaspoon salt

Preparation Method

Heat oven to 300° degrees. Beat butter, shortening and sugars in large bowl with electric mixer on medium speed, or mix with the spoon.

Stir in flour and salt. (Dough will be dry and crumbly; use hands to mix completely.)

Roll dough into rectangle, 15 × 7 1/2 inches, on lightly floured surface.

Cut into 1 1/2-inch squares. Place about 1 inch apart on ungreased cookie sheet.

Bake about 25 minutes or until set. (These cookies brown very little, and the shape does not change.) Remove from cookie sheet to wire rack.

Butterscotch-Oatmeal Crinkles

- ❖ 2 cups packed brown sugar

- ❖ 1/2 cup butter or margarine -- softened

- ❖ 1/2 cup shortening

- ❖ 1 teaspoon vanilla

- ❖ 2 eggs

- ❖ 2 1/4 cups all-purpose flour

- ❖ 2 cups old-fashioned or quick-cooking oats

- ❖ 1 1/2 teaspoons baking powder

- ❖ 1/2 teaspoon salt

- ❖ 1/2 cup granulated or powdered sugar

Preparation Method

Heat oven to 350°. Grease cookie sheet. Beat brown sugar, butter, shortening, vanilla and eggs in large bowl with electric mixer on medium speed, or mix with spoon. Stir in flour, oats, baking powder and salt.

Shape dough into 1-inch balls; roll in granulated sugar. Place about 2 inches apart on cookie sheet.

Bake 10 to 12 minutes or until almost no indentation remains when touched lightly in centre. Immediately remove from cookie sheet to wire rack.

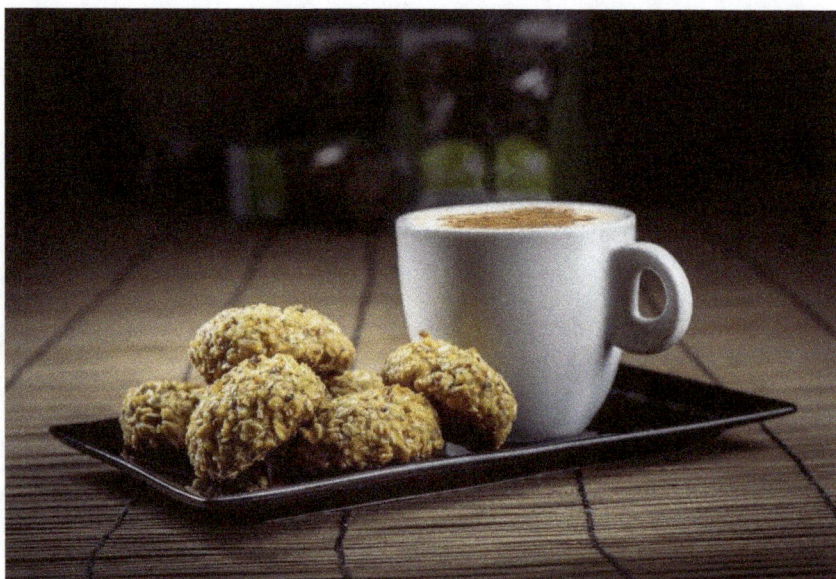

Candy Corn Shortbread

Amount Measure Ingredient

- ❖ 3/4 cup butter or margarine -- softened
- ❖ 1/4 cup sugar
- ❖ 2 cups all-purpose flour
- ❖ Yellow food color
- ❖ Red food color

Preparation Method

Beat butter and sugar in large bowl with electric mixer on medium speed or mix with spoon. Stir in flour. Divide dough into 6 equal parts.

Combine 3 parts dough; mix with 10 drops yellow food colour and 4 drops red food colour to make orange dough.

Combine 2 parts dough; mix with 7 drops yellow food colour to make yellow dough. Leave remaining part dough plain.

Pat orange dough into 3/4-inch-thick rectangle, 9 × 2 inches, on plastic wrap. Pat yellow dough into 1/2-inch-thick rectangle, 9 × 1 ¾ inches. Place yellow rectangle centred on orange rectangle. Shape plain dough into 9-inch roll, 3/4 inch in diameter. Place roll on centre of yellow rectangle.

Wrap plastic wrap around dough, pressing dough into triangle so that dough will resemble a kernel of corn when sliced.

Refrigerate about 2 hours or until firm.

Heat oven to 350°. Cut dough into 1/4-inch slices. Place about 1 inch apart on ungreased cookie sheet. Bake 10 to 12 minutes or until set.

Remove from cookie sheet to wire rack.

Stack dough so that the orange rectangle is on the bottom and the uncoloured roll of dough is on top.

Cappuccino-Pistachio Shortbread

Amount Measure Ingredient

- ❖ 2 tablespoons cappuccino-flavored instant coffee mix (dry)
- ❖ 1 tablespoon water
- ❖ 3/4 cup butter or margarine -- softened
- ❖ 1/2 cup powdered sugar
- ❖ 2 cups all-purpose flour
- ❖ 1/2 cup chopped pistachio nuts
- ❖ 1-ounce semisweet baking chocolate or white baking bar
- ❖ 1 teaspoon shortening

Preparation Method

Heat oven to 350°. Dissolve coffee mix in water in medium bowl. Add butter and powdered sugar.

Beat with electric mixer on medium speed until creamy or mix with a spoon. Stir in flour and nuts, using hands if necessary, until stiff dough forms.

Divide dough in half. Shape each half into a ball. Pat each ball into 6-inch round, about 1/2 inch thick, on lightly floured surface.

Cut each round into 16 wedges. Arrange wedges about 1/2 inch apart and with pointed ends toward centre on ungreased cookie sheet. Bake about 15 minutes or until golden brown.

Immediately remove from cookie sheet to wire rack. Cool completely.

Place chocolate and shortening in small microwavable bowl. Microwave uncovered on Medium (50%) 3 to 4 minutes, stirring after 2 minutes, until mixture can be stirred smooth and is thin enough to drizzle.

Drizzle over cookies.

Caramel Apple Cookies

Amount Measure Ingredient

- ❖ 1 cup sugar

- ❖ 1/2 cup butter or margarine -- softened

- ❖ 1/2 cup shortening

- ❖ 1 1/2 teaspoons vanilla

- ❖ 2 eggs

- ❖ 3 cups all-purpose flour

- ❖ 1/2 teaspoon baking soda

- ❖ 1/2 teaspoon salt

- ❖ Red paste food color, if desired

- ❖ About 24 wooden sticks with rounded ends

Caramel Glaze -- (recipe follows)

CARAMEL GLAZE

- ❖ 1 (14 ounce) package vanilla caramels

- ❖ 1/4 cup water

Preparation Method

Heat oven to 400°. Beat sugar, butter and shortening in large bowl with electric mixer on medium speed or mix with spoon.

Stir in vanilla and eggs. Stir in flour, baking soda and salt. Stir in food colour to tint dough red.

Roll dough 1/4 inch thick on lightly floured cloth-covered surface. Cut with 3-inch round or apple-shaped cookie cutter.

Place 2 inches apart on ungreased cookie sheet. Insert wooden stick into side of each cookie. Bake 8 to 9 minutes or until edges are light brown. Cool 2 minutes; remove from cookie sheet to wire rack. Cool completely.

Spread top third of each cookie (opposite wooden stick) with Caramel Glaze. Hold cookie upright to allow glaze to drizzle down cookie.

CARAMEL GLAZE:

Heat caramels and water in 2-quart saucepan over low heat, stirring frequently, until melted and smooth. If glaze becomes too stiff, heat over low heat, stirring constantly, until softened.

Caramel Candy Bars

Amount Measure Ingredient

- ❖ 1 (14 ounce) package vanilla caramels

- ❖ 1/3 cup milk

- ❖ 2 cups all-purpose flour

- ❖ 2 cups quick-cooking or old-fashioned oats

- ❖ 1 1/2 cups packed brown sugar

- ❖ 1 teaspoon baking soda

- ❖ 1/2 teaspoon salt

- ❖ 1 egg

- ❖ 1 cup butter or margarine -- softened

- ❖ 1 (6 ounce) package semisweet chocolate chips (1 cup)

- ❖ 1 cup chopped walnuts

OR

- ❖ 1 cup dry-roasted peanuts

Preparation Method

Heat oven to 350°. Heat caramels and milk in 2-quart saucepan over low heat, stirring frequently, until smooth; remove from the heat.

Mix flour, oats, brown sugar, baking soda and salt in large bowl with spoon. Stir in egg and butter until mixture is crumbly.

Press half of the crumbly mixture in ungreased rectangular pan, 13 × 9 × 2 inches.

Bake 10 minutes.

Sprinkle chocolate chips and walnuts over baked layer. Drizzle with caramel mixture. Sprinkle with remaining crumbly mixture; press gently into caramel mixture.

Bake 20 to 25 minutes or until golden brown. Cool 30 minutes.

Loosen edges from sides of pan. Cool completely. Cut into 8 rows by 4 rows.

Caramel Fudge Bars

Amount Measure Ingredient

❖ 1 package Supreme brownie mix (with

❖ pouch of Chocolate Flavor Syrup)

❖ 1/4 cup milk

❖ 1 teaspoon vanilla

❖ 1 egg

❖ 1/2 (14 ounce) package vanilla caramels (25 caramels)

❖ 1 (14 ounce) can sweetened condensed milk

Preparation Method

Heat oven to 350°. Grease bottom only of rectangular pan, 13 × 9 × 2 inches. Mix brownie mix (dry; do not add chocolate syrup from pouch), milk, vanilla and egg with spoon; reserve 1 cup. Press remaining brownie mixture in bottom of pan. Bake 10 minutes. Heat caramels and chocolate syrup from pouch in 2-quart saucepan over medium-low heat.

Stirring occasionally, until caramels are melted.

Stir in milk. Pour over baked layer. Break up reserved brownie mixture; sprinkle over caramel.

Bake 25 to 30 minutes or until bubbly around edges. Cool completely; refrigerate for easier cutting. Cut into 4 rows by 6 rows. Store tightly covered and, if desired, in refrigerator.

Caramel-Pecan Cookies

<u>**Amount Measure Ingredient**</u>

- ❖ 1/2 cup packed brown sugar
- ❖ 1/2 cup butter or margarine -- softened
- ❖ 2 tablespoons water
- ❖ 1 teaspoon vanilla
- ❖ 1 1/2 cups all-purpose flour
- ❖ 1/8 teaspoon salt
- ❖ 8 vanilla caramels
- ❖ 160 pecan halves (about 2 1/4 cups)

Chocolate Glaze -- (recipe follows)

CHOCOLATE GLAZE

- ❖ 1 ounce unsweetened baking chocolate
- ❖ 1 cup powdered sugar
- ❖ 1 teaspoon vanilla
- ❖ 2 teaspoons water (2 to 4 teaspoons)

Preparation Method

Heat oven to 350°. Beat brown sugar, butter, water and vanilla in large bowl with electric mixer on medium speed or mix with spoon. Stir in flour and salt.

Cut each caramel into 4 pieces with sharp knife. For each cookie, group 5 pecan halves on ungreased cookie sheet.

Shape 1 teaspoon dough around each caramel piece to form a ball. Press ball firmly onto centre of each group of pecans.

Bake 12 to 15 minutes or until set but not brown. Immediately remove from cookie sheet to wire rack. Cool completely.

Spread tops of cookies with Chocolate Glaze.

CHOCOLATE GLAZE:

Melt chocolate in 1-quart saucepan over low heat, stirring occasionally. Stir in powdered sugar, vanilla and water until smooth and spreadable.

Carrot-Molasses Cookies

Amount Measure Ingredient

❖ 1 package carrot cake mix

❖ 1/4 cup butter or margarine -- softened

❖ 2 tablespoons light molasses

❖ 2 eggs

❖ 1/2 cup chopped nuts, if desired

❖ 1 tub Rich & Creamy cream cheese

❖ ready-to-spread frosting, if desired

Preparation Method

Beat half of the cake mix (dry), the butter, molasses and eggs in large bowl with electric mixer on medium speed until smooth or mix with spoon. Stir in remaining cake mix and the nuts. Refrigerate about 2 hours or until chilled.

Heat oven to 375°. Lightly grease cookie sheet. Drop dough by rounded teaspoonfuls about 2 inches apart onto cookie sheet.

Bake 8 to 10 minutes or until edges are set (centres will be soft).

Remove from cookie sheet to wire rack. Cool completely. Frost with frosting. (Cover and refrigerate any remaining frosting.)

Carrot-Raisin Bars

Amount Measure Ingredient

❖ 1 package carrot cake mix

❖ 1/2 cup vegetable oil

❖ 1/4 cup water

❖ 2 eggs

❖ 3/4 cup raisins

❖ 1/2 cup chopped nuts

❖ 1 tub Rich & Creamy cream cheese

❖ frosting

Preparation Method

Heat oven to 350°. Grease and flour jelly roll pan, 15 1/2 × 10 1/2 × 1 inch. Mix cake mix (dry), oil, water and eggs in large bowl with spoon. Stir in raisins and nuts. Spread evenly in pan.

Bake 15 to 20 minutes or until bars spring back when touched lightly in centre. Cool completely. Frost with frosting. Cut into 8 rows by 6 rows.

Cherry-Almond Bars

Amount Measure Ingredient

- ❖ 1 (10 ounce) jar maraschino cherries
- ❖ 1 cup all-purpose flour
- ❖ 1/2 cup butter or margarine -- softened
- ❖ 1/4 cup powdered sugar
- ❖ 2 eggs
- ❖ 1 cup sliced almonds
- ❖ 1/2 cup granulated sugar
- ❖ 1/4 cup all-purpose flour
- ❖ 1/2 teaspoon baking powder

Pink Glaze -- (recipe follows)

PINK GLAZE

- ❖ 1/2 cup powdered sugar
- ❖ 1/4 teaspoon almond extract
- ❖ 2 teaspoons reserved maraschino cherry juice (2 to 3 teaspoons)

Preparation Method

Heat oven to 350°. Drain cherries, reserving juice for Pink Glaze. Chop cherries; set aside.

Mix 1 cup flour, the butter and powdered sugar with spoon. Press in ungreased square pan, 9 × 9 × 2 inches. Bake about 10 minutes or until set.

Beat eggs in medium bowl with fork. Stir in cherries and remaining ingredients except Pink Glaze.

Spread over baked layer. Bake 20 to 25 minutes or until golden brown. Cool completely.

Drizzle with Pink Glaze. Cut into 6 rows by 4 rows.

PINK GLAZE:

Mix all ingredients until smooth and thin enough to drizzle.

Chocolate Chip Cookies

Amount Measure Ingredient

- ❖ 1 package butter pecan,
- ❖ chocolate chip*, chocolate fudge, devil's food,
- ❖ German, chocolate or yellow cake mix
- ❖ 1/2 cup butter or margarine -- softened
- ❖ 1 teaspoon vanilla
- ❖ 2 eggs
- ❖ 1/2 cup chopped nuts
- ❖ 1 (6 ounce) package semisweet chocolate chips (1 cup)

Preparation Method

Heat oven to 350°. Beat half of cake mix (dry), butter, vanilla and eggs in large bowl with electric mixer on medium speed until smooth or mix with spoon.

Stir in remaining cake mix, the nuts and chocolate chips.

Drop dough by rounded teaspoonfuls about 2 inches apart onto ungreased cookie sheet.

Bake 10 to 12 minutes or until edges are set (centres will be soft). Cool 1 minute; remove from cookie sheet to wire rack.

Chocolate Chip Sandwich Cookies

Amount Measure Ingredient

- ❖ 1 1/4 cups packed brown sugar

- ❖ 1/2 cup butter or margarine -- softened

- ❖ 1 egg

- ❖ 1 1/4 cups all-purpose flour

- ❖ 1/4 teaspoon baking soda

- ❖ 1/8 teaspoon salt

- ❖ 1 cup miniature semisweet chocolate chips

Chocolate Frosting -- (recipe follows)

CHOCOLATE FROSTING

- ❖ 2 ounces unsweetened baking chocolate

- ❖ 2 tablespoons butter or margarine

- ❖ 2 cups powdered sugar

- ❖ 3 tablespoons hot water

Preparation Method

Heat oven to 350°. Lightly grease cookie sheet. Beat brown sugar, butter and egg in large bowl with electric mixer on medium speed or mix with spoon.

Stir in flour, baking soda and salt. Stir in chocolate chips.

Drop dough by level teaspoonfuls about 2 inches apart onto cookie sheet (dough will flatten and spread).

Bake 8 to 10 minutes or until golden brown. Cool 1 to 2 minutes; remove from cookie sheet to wire rack. Cool completely. Spread 1 teaspoon Chocolate Frosting between bottoms of pairs of cookies.

CHOCOLATE FROSTING:

Melt chocolate and butter in 2-quart saucepan over low heat, stirring occasionally; remove from heat. Stir in powdered sugar and hot water until smooth and spreadable.

(If frosting is too thick, add more water. If frosting is too thin, add more powdered sugar.)

Chocolate Chip-Pecan Bars

Amount Measure Ingredient

- ❖ 1 package French vanilla
- ❖ cake mix
- ❖ 1/2 cup butter or margarine -- softened
- ❖ 2 cups pecan halves
- ❖ 2/3 cup butter or margarine
- ❖ 1/2 cup packed brown sugar
- ❖ 1 (6 ounce) package semisweet chocolate chips (1 cup)

Preparation Method

Heat oven to 350°. Mix cake mix (dry) and 1/2 cup butter in a medium bowl, using pastry blender or crisscrossing 2 knives, until crumbly.

Press firmly in bottom of ungreased rectangular pan, 13 × 9 × 2 inches. Bake 8 to 10 minutes or until light brown.

Sprinkle pecan halves evenly over baked layer.

Heat 2/3 cup butter and the brown sugar to boiling in 2-quart saucepan over medium heat, stirring occasionally; boil and stir 1 minute. Spoon mixture evenly over pecans.

Bake about 20 minutes or until bubbly and light brown.

Sprinkle chocolate chips over warm bars; cool. Cut into 8 rows by 4 rows.

Chocolate Cookies

Amount Measure Ingredient

- ❖ 1 package ® devil's food
- ❖ cake mix
- ❖ 1/3 cup vegetable oil
- ❖ 2 eggs
- ❖ Sugar

Preparation Method

Heat oven to 350°. Mix cake mix (dry), oil and eggs in large bowl with spoon until dough forms.

Shape dough into 1-inch balls; roll in sugar. Place about 2 inches apart on ungreased cookie sheet.

Bake 8 to 10 minutes or until set. Remove from cookie sheet to wire rack.

Chocolate Drop Cookies

Amount Measure Ingredient

- ❖ 1 cup sugar

- ❖ 1/2 cup butter or margarine -- softened

- ❖ 1/3 cup buttermilk

- ❖ 1 teaspoon vanilla

- ❖ 2 ounces unsweetened baking chocolate -- melted and

- ❖ cooled

- ❖ 1 egg

- ❖ 1 3/4 cups all-purpose flour

- ❖ 1/2 teaspoon baking soda

- ❖ 1/2 teaspoon salt

- ❖ 1 cup chopped nuts

Chocolate Frosting -- (recipe follows)

CHOCOLATE FROSTING

- ❖ 2 ounces unsweetened baking chocolate

- ❖ 2 tablespoons butter or margarine

- ❖ 2 cups powdered sugar
- ❖ 3 tablespoons hot water

Preparation Method

Heat oven to 375°. Grease cookie sheet. Beat the sugar, butter, buttermilk, vanilla, chocolate, and egg in large bowl with an electric mixer on medium speed or mix with spoon. Stir in flour, baking soda and salt. Stir in nuts.

Drop dough by rounded tablespoonfuls about 2 inches apart onto cookie sheet. Bake 8 to 10 minutes or until almost no indentation remains when touched in centre.

Immediately remove from cookie sheet to wire rack. Cool completely. Frost with Chocolate Frosting.

CHOCOLATE FROSTING:

Melt chocolate and butter in 2-quart saucepan over low heat, stirring occasionally; remove from heat. Stir in powdered sugar and hot water until smooth and spreadable.

(If frosting is too thick, add more water. If frosting is too thin, add more powdered sugar.)

Chocolate Linzer Hearts

Amount Measure Ingredient

- ❖ 1 cup butter or margarine -- softened
- ❖ 1/2 cup sugar
- ❖ 1 teaspoon vanilla
- ❖ 2 eggs
- ❖ 1 cup hazelnuts -- toasted (see Notes), skinned and ground
- ❖ 1/2-ounce semisweet baking chocolate -- finely chopped
- ❖ 2 1/2 cups all-purpose flour
- ❖ 1 1/2 teaspoons ground cinnamon
- ❖ 1/2 teaspoon ground nutmeg
- ❖ 1/2 cup raspberry jam
- ❖ 1 ounce semisweet baking chocolate -- melted

Preparation Method

Beat butter and sugar in large bowl with electric mixer on medium speed until light and fluffy or mix with spoon.

Beat in vanilla and eggs until smooth. Add remaining ingredients except jam and melted chocolate.

Beat until well blended. Cover and refrigerate 1 hour (dough will be sticky).

Heat oven to 375°. Roll one fourth of dough at a time between pieces of waxed paper until 1/8 inch thick.

(Keep remaining dough refrigerated until ready to roll.)

Cut with 2-inch heart-shape cookie cutter. Cut small heart shape from centre of half of the 2-inch hearts, if desired. Place on ungreased cookie sheet.

Bake 7 to 9 minutes or until light brown. Remove from cookie sheet to wire rack. Cool completely.

Spread about 1/2 teaspoon raspberry jam on bottom of whole heart cookies: top with cut-out heart cookie.

Drizzle with melted chocolate. Let stand until chocolate is firm.

Chocolate Mini-Chippers

Amount Measure Ingredient

- ❖ 1/2 cup granulated sugar

- ❖ 1/4 cup packed brown sugar

- ❖ 1/4 cup butter or margarine -- softened

- ❖ 1 teaspoon vanilla

- ❖ 1 egg white

OR

- ❖ 2 tablespoons fat-free cholesterol-free egg product

- ❖ 1/2 cup all-purpose flour

- ❖ 1/2 cup whole wheat flour

- ❖ 1/2 teaspoon baking soda

- ❖ 1/4 teaspoon salt

- ❖ 1/2 cup miniature semisweet chocolate chips

Preparation Method

Heat oven to 375°. Beat sugars, butter, vanilla and egg white in large bowl with electric mixer on medium speed or mix with spoon. Stir in flours, baking soda and salt. Stir in chocolate chips. Drop dough by rounded teaspoonfuls about 2 inches apart onto ungreased cookie sheet.

Bake 8 to 10 minutes or until golden brown. Cool 1 to 2 minutes; remove from cookie sheet to wire rack.

Chocolate Shortbread

Amount Measure Ingredient

- ❖ 2 cups powdered sugar
- ❖ 1 1/2 cups butter or margarine -- softened
- ❖ 3 cups all-purpose flour
- ❖ 3/4 cup baking cocoa
- ❖ 2 teaspoons vanilla
- ❖ 4 ounces semisweet baking chocolate -- melted and cooled
- ❖ 1/2 teaspoon shortening

Creamy Frosting -- (recipe follows)

CREAMY FROSTING

- ❖ 3 cups powdered sugar
- ❖ 1/3 cup butter or margarine -- softened
- ❖ 1 1/2 teaspoons vanilla
- ❖ 2 tablespoons (about) milk

Preparation Method

Heat oven to 325°. Beat powdered sugar and butter in large bowl with electric mixer on medium speed until light and fluffy or mix with spoon. Stir in flour, cocoa and vanilla.

Roll half of dough at a time 1/2 inch thick on lightly floured surface.

Cut into 3-inch rounds. Place 2 inches apart on ungreased cookie sheet. Bake 9 to 11 minutes or until firm (cookies should not be dark brown). Remove from cookie sheet to wire rack. Cool completely.

Mix chocolate and shortening until smooth. Prepare Creamy Frosting.

Spread each cookie with about 1 teaspoon frosting.

Immediately make three concentric circles on frosting with melted chocolate.

Starting at centre, draw a toothpick through chocolate circles to make spider web design. Let stand until chocolate is firm.

CREAMY FROSTING:

Mix powdered sugar and butter in medium bowl. Stir in vanilla and milk. Beat with spoon until smooth and spreadable.

Chocolate-Almond Tea Cakes

Amount Measure Ingredient

- ❖ 3/4 cup butter or margarine -- softened
- ❖ 1/3 cup powdered sugar
- ❖ 1 1/4 cups all-purpose flour
- ❖ 1/2 cup hot cocoa mix (dry)
- ❖ 1/2 cup chopped slivered almonds -- toasted (see Notes)
- ❖ Powdered sugar

Preparation Method

Heat oven to 325°. Beat butter and 1/3 cup powdered sugar in medium bowl with electric mixer on medium speed or mix with spoon. Stir in flour, cocoa mix, and almonds. (If dough is soft, cover and refrigerate until firm enough to shape.)

Shape dough into 1-inch balls. Place 2 inches apart on ungreased cookie sheet. Bake 12 to 15 minutes or until set.

Dip tops into powdered sugar while warm. Cool completely on wire rack. Dip tops into powdered sugar again.

Chocolate-Bourbon Balls

Amount Measure Ingredient

- ❖ 1 (9 ounce) package chocolate wafer cookies -- finely crushed (2
- ❖ 1/3 cups)
- ❖ 2 cups finely chopped almonds
- ❖ 2 cups powdered sugar
- ❖ 1/4 cup bourbon
- ❖ 1/4 cup light corn syrup
- ❖ Powdered sugar

Preparation Method

Mix crushed cookies, almonds and 2 cups powdered sugar in large bowl. Stir in bourbon and corn syrup.

Shape mixture into 1-inch balls. Roll in powdered sugar. Cover tightly and refrigerate at least 5 days to blend flavours.

Chocolate-Cherry Sand Tarts

Amount Measure Ingredient

- ❖ 3/4 cup sugar

- ❖ 3/4 cup butter or margarine -- softened

- ❖ 1 egg white

- ❖ 1 3/4 cups all-purpose flour

- ❖ 1/4 cup baking cocoa

- ❖ 1 3/4 cups (about) cherry preserves

Chocolate Drizzle -- (recipe follows)

CHOCOLATE DRIZZLE

- ❖ 2/3 cup semisweet chocolate chips

- ❖ 1 tablespoon shortening

Preparation Method

Beat sugar, butter and egg white in large bowl with electric mixer on medium speed or mix with spoon. Stir in flour and cocoa.

Cover and refrigerate about 2 hours or until firm.

Heat oven to 350°. Shape dough into 1-inch balls.

Press each ball in bottom and upside of each ungreased sandbakelse mold, about 1 ¾ × 1/2 inch.

Spoon about 1 1/2 teaspoons cherry preserves into each mold. Place on cookie sheet.

Bake 12 to 15 minutes or until crust is set. Cool 10 minutes; carefully remove from molds to wire rack. Cool completely.

Drizzle with Chocolate Drizzle.

CHOCOLATE DRIZZLE:

Melt ingredients over low heat, stirring occasionally, until smooth.

Chocolate-Covered Peanut-Chocolate Chip Cookies

Amount Measure Ingredient

- ❖ 1 cup sugar
- ❖ 1/2 cup butter or margarine -- softened
- ❖ 1/2 cup shortening
- ❖ 1 teaspoon vanilla
- ❖ 1 egg
- ❖ 1 3/4 cups all-purpose flour
- ❖ 1/2 teaspoon baking soda
- ❖ 1/4 teaspoon salt
- ❖ 1 cup chocolate-covered peanuts
- ❖ 1 cup milk chocolate chips

Preparation Method

Heat oven to 375°. Beat sugar, butter, shortening, vanilla and egg in large bowl with electric mixer on medium speed, or mix with spoon.

Stir in flour, baking soda and salt. Stir in peanuts and chocolate chips.

Drop dough by rounded tablespoonfuls about 2 inches apart onto ungreased cookie sheet.

Bake 10 to 12 minutes or until edges are golden brown (centres will be soft). Cool 1 to 2 minutes; remove from cookie sheet to wire rack.

Chocolate-Glazed Graham Crackers

Amount Measure Ingredient

- ❖ 1 cup shortening

- ❖ 1/2 cup packed brown sugar

- ❖ 1/4 cup honey

- ❖ 2 cups whole wheat flour

- ❖ 1/2 teaspoon baking powder

- ❖ 1/4 teaspoon salt

- ❖ 1/2 cup semisweet chocolate chips

- ❖ 1 tablespoon shortening

Preparation Method

Heat oven to 375°. Beat 1 cup shortening, the brown sugar and honey in large bowl with electric mixer on medium speed or mix with spoon.

Stir in flour, baking powder and salt.

Roll half of dough at a time 1/8 inch thick on lightly floured cloth-covered surface. Cut into 2 1/2-inch rounds.

Place 1 inch apart on ungreased cookie sheet. Bake 7 to 9 minutes or until edges are firm.

Cool 1 to 2 minutes; remove from cookie sheet to wire rack. Cool completely.

Melt chocolate chips and 1 tablespoon shortening over low heat, stirring occasionally, until smooth.

Drizzle over cookies.

Chocolate-Mint Cookies

Amount Measure Ingredient

- ❖ 1 cup sugar

- ❖ 1/2 cup butter or margarine -- softened

- ❖ 1 teaspoon vanilla

- ❖ 1 egg

- ❖ 2 (1 ounce) squares unsweetened chocolate -- melted and cooled

- ❖ 1 cup all-purpose flour

- ❖ 1/2 teaspoon salt

Peppermint Frosting -- (recipe follows)

- ❖ 1/4 cup butter or margarine

- ❖ 2 tablespoons corn syrup

- ❖ 1 (6 ounce) package semisweet chocolate chips

- ❖ Crushed hard peppermint candies, if desired

PEPPERMINT FROSTING

- ❖ 2 1/2 cups powdered sugar

- ❖ 1/4 cup butter or margarine -- softened
- ❖ 3 tablespoons milk
- ❖ 1/2 teaspoon peppermint extract

Preparation Method

Heat oven to 375°. Beat sugar, 1/2 cup butter, the vanilla, egg and unsweetened chocolate in large bowl with electric mixer on medium speed or mix with spoon. Stir in flour and salt.

Drop dough by rounded teaspoonfuls about 2 inches apart onto ungreased cookie sheet. Flatten cookies with greased bottom of glass dipped in sugar. Bake until set, about 8 minutes. Cool 1 to 2 minutes; remove from cookie sheet to wire rack. Cool cookies completely.

Spread Peppermint Frosting over each cookie to within 1/4 inch of edge. Melt 1/4 cup butter, the corn syrup and chocolate chips over low heat, stirring constantly, until smooth. Spoon or drizzle mixture over each cookie; sprinkle with crushed candies.

PEPPERMINT FROSTING:

Mix all ingredients until smooth and of spreading consistency.

Chocolate-Oatmeal Chewies

Amount Measure Ingredient

- ❖ 1 1/2 cups sugar

- ❖ 1 cup butter or margarine -- softened

- ❖ 1/4 cup milk

- ❖ 1 egg

- ❖ 2 2/3 cups quick-cooking or old-fashioned oats

- ❖ 1 cup all-purpose flour

- ❖ 1/2 cup baking cocoa

- ❖ 1/2 teaspoon salt

- ❖ 1/2 teaspoon baking soda

Preparation Method

Heat oven to 350°. Beat sugar, butter, milk and egg in large bowl with electric mixer on medium speed, or mix with spoon. Stir in remaining ingredients.

Drop dough by rounded tablespoonfuls about 2 inches apart onto ungreased cookie sheet.

Bake 10 to 12 minutes or until almost no indentation remains when touched in centre.

Cool 1 to 2 minutes; remove from cookie sheet to wire rack.

Chocolate-Orange-Chocolate Chip Cookies

Amount Measure Ingredient

- ❖ 1 cup sugar
- ❖ 2/3 cup butter or margarine -- softened
- ❖ 1 tablespoon grated orange peel
- ❖ 1 egg
- ❖ 1 1/2 cups all-purpose flour
- ❖ 1/3 cup baking cocoa
- ❖ 1/4 teaspoon salt
- ❖ 1/4 teaspoon baking powder
- ❖ 1/4 teaspoon baking soda
- ❖ 1 cup chopped pecans
- ❖ 1 (6 ounce) package semisweet chocolate morsels (1 cup)
- ❖ 1/3 cup sugar
- ❖ 1 teaspoon grated orange peel

Preparation Method

Heat oven to 350°. Beat 1 cup sugar, butter, 1 tablespoon grated orange peel and the egg in large bowl with electric mixer on medium speed or mix with spoon.

Stir in flour, cocoa, salt, baking powder and baking soda. Stir in pecans and chocolate morsels.

Shape dough into 1 1/2-inch balls. Mix 1/3 cup sugar and 1 teaspoon grated orange peel. Roll balls in sugar mixture.

Place about 3 inches apart on ungreased cookie sheet. Flatten to about 1/2-inch thickness with bottom of glass.

Bake 9 to 11 minutes or until set. Cool slightly; remove from cookie sheet. Cool on wire rack.

Chocolate-Peanut Butter No-Bakes

Amount Measure Ingredient

- ❖ 1 (6 ounce) package semisweet chocolate chips (1 cup)
- ❖ 1/4 cup light corn syrup
- ❖ 1/4 cup peanut butter
- ❖ 2 tablespoons milk
- ❖ 1 teaspoon vanilla
- ❖ 2 cups quick-cooking oats
- ❖ 1 cup peanuts

Preparation Method

Cover cookie sheet with waxed paper. Heat chocolate chips, corn syrup, peanut butter, milk and vanilla in 3-quart saucepan over medium heat, stirring constantly, until chocolate is melted, and mixture is smooth; remove from heat.

Stir in oats and peanuts until well coated.

Drop mixture by rounded tablespoonfuls onto waxed paper.

Refrigerate uncovered about 1 hour or until firm. Store covered in refrigerator.

Chocolate-Peanut Windmills

Amount Measure Ingredient

❖ 1 cup sugar

❖ 1/4 cup butter or margarine -- softened

❖ 1/4 cup shortening

❖ 1/2 teaspoon vanilla

❖ 1 egg

❖ 2 ounces unsweetened baking chocolate -- melted and cooled

❖ 1 3/4 cups all-purpose flour

❖ 1 teaspoon baking powder

❖ 1/8 teaspoon salt

❖ 1/2 cup finely chopped peanuts

Preparation Method

Beat sugar, butter, shortening, vanilla and egg in large bowl with electric mixer on medium speed, or mix with spoon. Stir in chocolate.

Stir in flour, baking powder and salt. Cover and refrigerate about 2 hours or until firm.

Heat oven to 400°. Divide dough in half. Roll each half into rectangle, 12 × 9 inches, on lightly floured cloth-covered surface.

Sprinkle each rectangle with half of the peanuts; gently press into dough. Cut dough into 3-inch squares.

Place about 2 inches apart on ungreased cookie sheet.

Cut squares diagonally from each corner almost to centre. Fold every other point to centre to resemble pinwheel.

Bake about 6 minutes or until set. Remove from cookie sheet to wire rack.

Cut squares diagonally from each corner almost to centre.

Fold every other point to centre to resemble pinwheel.

Chocolate-Pecan Squares

Amount Measure Ingredient

- ❖ 1 cup all-purpose flour

- ❖ 1/2 cup packed brown sugar

- ❖ 3 tablespoons butter or margarine -- softened

- ❖ 1/2 cup packed brown sugar

- ❖ 1/2 cup butter or margarine

- ❖ 1 cup chopped pecans

- ❖ 1 teaspoon vanilla

- ❖ 1/2 cup semisweet chocolate chips

Preparation Method

Heat oven to 350°. Beat flour, 1/2 cup brown sugar and 3 tablespoons butter with electric mixer on low speed until blended.

Beat on medium speed 1 to 2 minutes or until crumbly.

Press evenly in bottom of ungreased square pan, 9 × 9 × 2 or 8 × 8 × 2 inches.

Cook 1/2 cup brown sugar and 1/2 cup butter over medium heat, stirring constantly, until mixture begins to boil.

Boil and stir 1 minute.

Stir in pecans and vanilla. Pour over layer in pan.

Bake 18 to 20 minutes or until topping is bubbly. Sprinkle evenly with chocolate chips.

Bake 2 minutes longer to soften chocolate (do not spread). Cool 10 minutes; loosen edges with knife. Cool completely.

Cut into 6 rows by 6 rows. Store covered in the refrigerator.

Chocolate-Peppermint Refrigerator Cookies

Amount Measure Ingredient

- ❖ 1 1/2 cups powdered sugar
- ❖ 1 cup butter or margarine -- softened
- ❖ 1 egg
- ❖ 2 2/3 cups all-purpose flour
- ❖ 1/4 teaspoon salt
- ❖ 1/4 cup baking cocoa
- ❖ 1 tablespoon milk
- ❖ 1/4 cup finely crushed hard peppermint candy

Preparation Method

Beat powdered sugar, butter and egg in large bowl with electric mixer on medium speed or mix with spoon. Stir in flour and salt. Divide dough in half. Stir cocoa and milk into one half and peppermint candy into another half.

Roll or pat chocolate dough into rectangle, 12 × 6 1/2 inches, on waxed paper.

Shape peppermint dough into roll, 12 inches long; place on chocolate dough.

Wrap chocolate dough around peppermint dough, using waxed paper to help lift. Press edges together.

Wrap and refrigerate about 2 hours or until firm.

Heat oven to 375°. Cut roll into 1/4-inch slices. Place about 1 inch apart on ungreased cookie sheet.

Bake 8 to 10 minutes or until set.

Remove from cookie sheet to wire rack.

CPSIA information can be obtained
at www.ICGtesting.com
Printed in the USA
BVHW011515030321
601595BV00001B/19

9 781914 405501